WHAT YOU SHOULD KNOW ABOUT . . .

MONSTERS

T5-AFO-019

Table of Contents

by Nancy White

What You Should Know About . . . SERIES

The Facts About Monsters

Seeing is believing, right?

Wrong! Plenty of people claim to have seen monsters, such as space aliens, Bigfoot, and the Loch Ness (pronounced *lock ness*) monster. Some of these people have photos and videos to back up their claims. You might even see something yourself that looks like a monster. Even so, scientists and most other people know that monster stories are the products of active imaginations.

Most monster sightings can be explained in one of two ways. One is that people see something they *think* is a monster, but it is really something else. For example, the "sea monster" out in the water is really a floating log. The "space alien" is really a house cat with a glow-in-the-dark collar.

Another explanation is that some people like the attention they get from pulling a **hoax**—creating fake evidence to trick others. A video of Bigfoot on the Internet just shows a person in a costume.

Even though monsters don't exist, they're fun to imagine. Maybe that's because life with monsters is more exciting than everyday real life. So go ahead and enjoy a scary monster movie. Just remember that the monsters are only special effects.

In addition, do some research and reading about monsters. (Check out some of the books on page 32.) You may find that the facts about how a monster story got started can be as interesting as the story itself.

On Sunday, October 30, 1938, thousands of people in the United States panicked when they heard on the radio that Martians were attacking Earth. Some people ran screaming from their homes. Radio and police stations were flooded with calls from listeners asking how to protect themselves.

The terrified listeners had tuned in too late to hear the introduction to the show, which explained that what they were hearing was not a news report. It was a radio play based on one of the most popular science fiction books of all time—*War of the Worlds,* by the famous British author H. G. Wells.

What happened that day back in 1938 is a perfect example of what happens when people believe what they hear without knowing the facts.

H·G·WELLS'
THE *War* OF THE *Worlds*

COLOR BY TECHNICOLOR
PRODUCED BY GEORGE PAL · DIRECTED BY BYRON HASKIN · SCREEN PLAY BY BARRE LYNDON · A PARAMOUNT PICTURE

Many people who report having seen UFOs or aliens provide photos to back up their claims. This image has been digitally altered so that UFOs appear to be flying overhead.

The belief that space aliens have visited Earth is still going strong. On April 24, 1964, an American police officer in New Mexico, U.S.A., reported seeing two small creatures standing next to a landed spacecraft. On November 24, 1978, a man in Italy claimed he had been attacked by small space aliens with yellow skin, huge ears, and fanglike teeth. On March 22, 2009, an American couple said they witnessed three "beings" step out of a disc-shaped UFO (unidentified flying object) near a highway in Texas.

Many reports of alien sightings have been investigated, but not one of them has been **validated**, or proven to be true. Also, most scientists do not believe that aliens have visited Earth. These two facts should make people **skeptical** about space alien stories.

In 2001, Charlie Tolbert, president of the Society of Scientific Exploration in the United States, said that all reported UFO sightings had "been explainable." For example, one reported UFO turned out to be the planet Venus sitting low in the night sky. Another was a cat at night wearing a light-up collar. Still another was a blimp. (Many people mistake blimps for UFOs because at night a blimp can look like a disc within a circle of lights.)

In addition to UFO reports that are mistakes, there are also out-and-out hoaxes. Some people have shown photos of "aliens" that they created using basic computer software.

Images of aliens can be created with basic computer software.

The most famous reports of a UFO and space aliens date back to 1947, when many people believed that **wreckage** found in Roswell, New Mexico, U.S.A., was a crashed UFO. Some even claimed that they saw dead aliens from the crash.

An official U.S. government report identified the wreckage as military equipment carried by balloons to detect nuclear explosions. The report also explained that the "aliens" were dummies dropped from balloons to test parachutes for military pilots. Some people, however, are still convinced that a spaceship crashed in Roswell.

For years, scientists from SETI (Search for **Extraterrestrial** Intelligence) in the United States have been searching the skies for signs of extraterrestrial life. To sum up their conclusions, here's what they have to say: "Have we found aliens? No, not yet."

Each year, the town of Roswell, New Mexico, U.S.A., holds a UFO Festival, which includes an alien pet costume contest.

The Loch Ness Monster

More than 4,000 people have claimed that they have seen a monster in Loch Ness, a large lake in Scotland. The "beast" has been photographed, filmed, and described in newspapers. Although none of the evidence has been validated, many people think the creature is real. It even has a nickname—"Nessie."

People say that Nessie is as long as a bus and weighs as much as two elephants. They also describe her as dark grey with a humped back, flippers, and a long curving neck.

Near Loch Ness are a visitors' center, a hotel, and restaurants for Nessie's many fans, who pay for a tour or a boat ride, hoping for a glimpse—and a photo—of their favorite monster.

Nessie sightings have a long history. The earliest one was 1,400 years ago. A monk claimed that he saved the life of a swimmer who was being threatened by a large beast. The monk commanded the monster to "go back with all speed," and it disappeared into the lake.

Nessie started making headlines in 1933, when a newspaper reported that an "enormous animal" had been spotted in Loch Ness. A hunter who was hired to find the beast claimed that he had found its tracks, but scientists proved the footprints were phony. They had been made with the dried foot of a dead hippopotamus.

Nessie made a comeback in 1934 in a photo, supposedly taken by a British doctor, Robert Wilson. It showed what looked like a monster rising out of Loch Ness. Many people suspected that the photo was a hoax, but they were not proved right until 1994, when a friend of Wilson's admitted that he had made the "monster" out of a toy submarine and then had it photographed. Wilson pretended that he took the photo because people were more likely to believe the story if a doctor told it.

This 1934 photo of Nessie, supposedly taken by Robert Wilson, a doctor, was one of the world's greatest hoaxes.

Someone hoping to see the Loch Ness monster could get excited and think this object in the water was Nessie.

Despite many people's doubts, others continued to search for and even "see" Nessie. All the sightings had simple explanations, however, such as waves, logs floating in the water, or swimming deer. Then, in 1987, a group of Nessie hunters launched an all-out search of Loch Ness. It was called Operation Deepscan. Twenty-four boats equipped with high-tech equipment that cost one million British pounds (about 3.6 million U.S. dollars today) failed to come up with a monster.

In spite of the exposed hoaxes, unproven claims, and failed searches, people will probably go on "seeing" Nessie. Maybe they're willing to believe a floating log is a mysterious lake monster because it's entertaining to believe that a favorite story could be true. It's important, however, to remember that there's a difference between fact and fiction.

It's huge, it's hairy, and it looks like a giant, apelike man—or a giant, manlike ape. It lives in the mountains and forests of the northwestern United States, Nepal, India, and Siberia. Many people have seen the gigantic footprints that gave the creature its name—Bigfoot—though it is also called Sasquatch and Yeti. Some have seen Bigfoot itself and even captured it on film. No bones or bodies of a Bigfoot have ever been found, however. That's because Bigfoot does not exist.

Like the Loch Ness monster, Bigfoot has many believers who point to photos or videos of the creature as proof that it's real. None of the evidence has been validated, however, and most "proofs" of Bigfoot's existence have been shown to be hoaxes.

One of the biggest hoaxes was revealed in 2002. A man had made "Bigfoot" tracks for years, wearing a pair of 16-inch (41-centimeter) wooden feet. Samples of Bigfoot hair have turned out to be from an elk, bear, or cow. And Bigfoot blood has been identified as transmission fluid from a car. An American film made in California, U.S.A., shows "Bigfoot" walking in the woods, but a professor of **anthropology** at the University of Washington stated that it was "just a man in a costume."

An article in *USA Today*, printed in May 1996, says, "In the scientific community, Bigfoot is usually good for a few laughs." The article goes on to quote a **zoologist** from Washington State University as saying, "There is no such thing as Bigfoot."

A man dressed up as Bigfoot for a movie shot on a mountain in New Hampshire, U.S.A.

Frankenstein is a doctor who creates a monster in a novel by the English writer Mary Shelley. The story of how Shelley came up with the idea is almost as interesting as the monster tale itself.

In the summer of 1816, Shelley and some of her friends were taking a vacation in the mountains in Switzerland. One rainy night, they decided to have a contest to see who could write the scariest horror story. Shelley won with her book *Frankenstein*. It was published and became an instant bestseller. Now, around 200 years later, it is still a classic.

In the novel, a young scientist named Victor Frankenstein wants to discover the secret of life, and he creates a monster out of dead body parts. Horrified by the monster's ugliness, Victor runs from his laboratory, and the monster escapes. Out in the world, the monster wants only to be accepted by humans. But, because of his hideous appearance, he is feared and shunned by everyone.

Suffering from rejection and loneliness, the monster begins to hate and murder humans. Victor spends the rest of his life trying to kill his creation. Finally, Victor dies of an illness, and the monster, grieving for his creator and feeling sorry for his crimes, destroys himself.

The monster in the story doesn't have a name, but even with the wrong name, he is one of the most unforgettable characters in monster history.

The first movie based on *Frankenstein* was a black-and-white silent film made in 1910. The monster has been a star of scary movies ever since.

There is no such thing as a zombie. In **folklore**, a zombie is a person who has died and come back to life. Zombies are not like normal, living people. They have no thoughts or will of their own. Their only concern seems to be eating people—or just their brains. Of course, zombies can't be killed, because they're already dead.

Zombies come mostly from TV shows, graphic novels, and countless zombie films, including the all-time zombie classic, *Night of the Living Dead*. These stories have made the zombie one of the public's favorite monsters.

Everyone should know that bringing a dead person—or a dead anything—back to life is scientifically impossible. Yet, many people enjoy joking about a "zombie **apocalypse**," or all-out zombie attack, taking place one day. There are "zombie fitness" workouts that get people physically fit to run away from zombies—just to have fun while exercising.

The U.S. government even created a website and a graphic novel teaching people how to prepare for a zombie apocalypse. It was a humorous way to explain how to prepare for any kind of disaster.

Since zombies do not exist, however, a zombie attack is one thing to cross off your list of things to worry about.

"They're coming to get you, Barbara!" That's a famous line from *Night of the Living Dead*, the 1968 horror movie classic that brought zombies to stardom.

Mummies That Come to Life

There's one thing about mummies that makes them different from the other monsters in this book. They are real. The ancient Egyptians mummified or preserved the bodies of their **pharaohs**. Ancient mummies have also been found in China and in other countries all over the world.

Methods of mummy-making differed from one culture to another. The Egyptians removed the **organs** from the body, dried the body in salt, and wrapped it in linen. People of Papua New Guinea, "smoked" dead bodies over a fire for about thirty days.

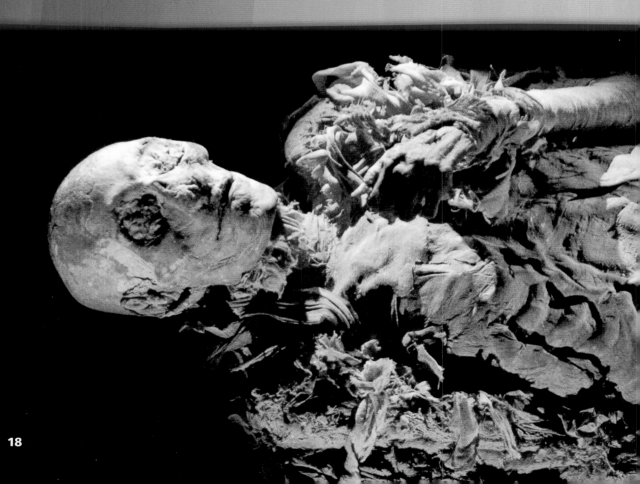

Mummies are important because they help us learn about ancient cultures. For example, the clothes and jewelry worn by mummies tell us how people dressed. Their bodies can tell what kinds of diseases killed them.

So mummies are nothing to be afraid of. At some point, however, someone got the idea that a mummy could come back to life as a scary monster. The movie *The Mummy*, filmed in 1932, started the real mummy craze. It was followed by *The Mummy's Tomb*, *The Mummy's Hand*, *The Mummy's Curse*…you get the picture.

Mummy monster movies can be fun to watch, but the same fact applies to mummies that applies to zombies: dead people cannot return to life.

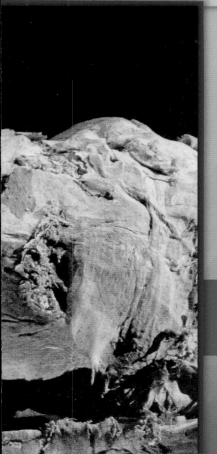

This mummy is the female pharaoh Hatshepsut, who ruled ancient Egypt 3,500 years ago.

Mermaids

Many people today know about mermaids from the Walt Disney movie *The Little Mermaid*. The movie is based on a story by the nineteenth-century Danish author Hans Christian Andersen. In both the story and the movie, a beautiful, kind mermaid saves a shipwrecked prince from drowning and falls in love with him.

But before Andersen wrote his tale, most people would have described mermaids differently. In older stories, mermaids used their beautiful songs to lure sailors to wreck their ships against rocks or jump overboard and drown.

The Little Mermaid from Hans Christian Andersen's *Fairy Tales*, published in 1900

Although mermaid stories go back a long time, mermaids are not real. That fact didn't keep people from being fooled by fakes. One famous mermaid hoax was pulled off in the nineteenth century by P. T. Barnum, the founder of the Ringling Bros. and Barnum and Bailey Circus in America. Barnum charged people to see what he said was the body of a mermaid. Crowds lined up to take a look at the hideous creature, which turned out to be parts of a dead monkey and a fish sewn together.

P. T. Barnum called his hoax the "Feejee Mermaid."

In 2012, the American TV channel Animal Planet aired a show called *Mermaids: The Body Found*. It showed a fake video of a man finding a mermaid on a beach, but some viewers thought it was real. A science writer for the magazine *Wired* criticized the show, calling it "rot." He felt it was wrong for the show to present a fictional story as though it were true. "It's not surprising that some viewers were confused about what they were actually seeing," the writer said.

For ideas about how the mermaid myth began, *Science World* magazine interviewed Laurel Kendall, an anthropologist who helped create an exhibit

A dugong (surrounded by some fish) heads to the surface to breathe.

called "Mythic Creatures: Dragons, Unicorns, and Mermaids" at the American Museum of Natural History in New York. Kendall said that marine mammals called dugongs may have started the belief in mermaids.

Dugongs, like all mammals, need air, so they come to the surface of the water to breathe.

Ancient sailors may have seen them surfacing and mistaken them for mermaids because dugongs have flippers and tails and move gracefully through the water. It seems like a stretch of the imagination to mistake a dugong for a mermaid, but it's amazing what people will believe if they let their imaginations stretch.

This dragon sits atop a temple in Taipei, Taiwan.

Dragons in art and stories date back thousands of years, to the very beginning of human civilization. Long ago, people thought that dragons were real. In fact, up until the early eighteenth century, dragons appeared in eyewitness accounts and even in scientific books about natural history. Around 300 years ago, scientists learned more, and people finally understood that dragons are creatures of myth.

Dragons do not exist, nor have they ever existed. And yet, images of dragons from ancient times can be seen all over the world, and they are all similar. Myths from ancient Greece and Rome feature dragons. The beasts are also found in Egyptian hieroglyphs, on Chinese scrolls, on the walls of Aztec temples, and on the **prows** of Viking ships. What made ancient people from different cultures dream up the same nonexistent creature?

One explanation is that dragons combine everything people have feared since the earliest humans walked the earth. A towering, fire-breathing, flying, snakelike monster with teeth like daggers was everyone's worst nightmare.

Another explanation has to do with fossils. Long before scientists learned about dinosaurs, people around the world found the bones of dinosaurs and other **extinct** animals. The bones obviously came from creatures that were different from and much larger than any animal living at the time. It's possible that dragon myths were based on these fossil finds.

Scientific explanations should not spoil the fun of reading stories and seeing movies about dragons. As Peter Hogarth, a dragon expert, said in an online interview, real dragons live in only one place— "where they always have lived, in people's imaginations!"

This statue of a dragon sits on a bridge in Slovenia.

According to folklore, a werewolf is a man who turns into a wolf or into a humanlike creature with a wolf's head and fur. In some werewolf stories, the change occurs during the full moon or if the man puts on a magic belt made of wolf skin. When in wolf mode, the werewolf is large, swift, strong, and out to kill.

Back in the 1500s, many people believed werewolves were real. This was unfortunate—in fact, it was tragic. People accused of being werewolves were horribly tortured and even killed.

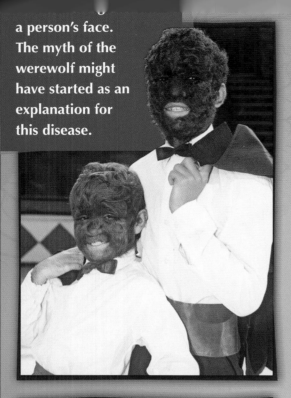

a person's face. The myth of the werewolf might have started as an explanation for this disease.

As with many other monster tales, werewolf stories can be explained with facts. For example, a rare disease called hypertrichosis (hy-per-trih-CO-sis) causes thick hair to grow on a person's face, giving him a wolf-like appearance. Another example is a disease called rabies, which can cause dogs and wolves to attack, bite, and even kill humans. Hundreds of years ago, people may have thought these infected animals were werewolves.

Now everyone knows—or *should* know—that it is impossible for somebody to change into an animal . . . or into anything at all, for that matter. But the story of what happened to people accused of being werewolves is a good example of the harm that can be caused by believing without thinking.

Diseased wolves on the attack may have looked like werewolves to terrified villagers.

When someone claims to have seen a monster, how can you tell whether the claim is true or not? First, think about it. Ask yourself if the claim makes sense. Second, do some research. See what scientists and other experts have to say. Find out how the story of the monster got started in the first place. You'll learn that no monster sighting has ever been validated. They are either mistakes, the results of someone's overactive imagination, or out-and-out hoaxes.

So use your head and the research tools available to you, and you'll come to the right conclusion. Monster stories are pure fiction. The fact is that monsters don't exist—but they do offer great material for some spine-chilling stories.

anthropology (an-thruh-PAH-luh-jee) n., the study of ways in which different people around the world live

apocalypse (uh-PAW-kuh-lips) n., the total destruction of the world

extinct (ik-STINKT) adj., having died out

extraterrestrial (ek-struh-tuh-RES-tree-uhl) adj., from a planet other than Earth

folklore (FOHK-lawr) n., stories and beliefs passed down through many generations

hoax (HOHKS) n., a trick that makes an event or object look like something else

organs (AWR-guhns) n., parts of the body that have particular functions

pharaohs (FER-ohs) n., rulers of ancient Egypt

prows (PROWS) n., the front parts of ships

skeptical (SKEP-ti-kuhl) adj., doubtful; reluctant to believe something

validated (VA-luh-day-tuhd) adj., based on facts or evidence

wreckage (REH-kij) n., broken parts or pieces found at the site of a crash or explosion

zoologist (zew-AW-luh-jist) n., a scientist who studies animal life

Index

Bibliography

DK Publishing. *Children's Book of Mythical Beasts and Magical Monsters.* DK Children, 2011.

Drake, Dr. Ernest. *Monsterology: The Complete Book of Monstrous Beasts.* Candlewick, 2008.

Gee, Joshua. *Encyclopedia Horrifica: The Terrifying TRUTH! About Vampires, Ghosts, Monsters, and More.* Scholastic, 2007.

Kelly, Sophia. *What a Beast!: A Look-It-Up Guide to the Monsters and Mutants of Mythology.* Franklin Watts, 2009.

Regan, Lisa. *Vampires, Werewolves & Zombies.* Scholastic Books, 2009.

Shuker, Karl P. N. *Dragons: A Natural History.* Simon & Schuster, 1995.

Wallace, Holly. *Can Science Solve?: The Mystery of the Abominable Snowman.* Heinemann-Raintree, 2006.